The Most Powerful Quotes to Enhance Your Life

Over 500 original quotes to sip, savor, and share!

Inspirational and Motivational Quotations to Strengthen Your Mental, Physical, and Spiritual Health

Kala Jordan-Lindsey

The Most Powerful Quotes to Enhance Your Life

Copyright © 2022 by Kala Jordan-Lindsey

All rights reserved. No portion of this book may be reproduced or utilized in any form or by any means, electronic or mechanical, including photocopying, recording, or by any other information storage and retrieval system, without permission in writing from the author.

Disclaimer

This book is not intended as a substitute for medical advice of physicians. The reader should regularly consult a physician in matters relating to his/her health and particularly with respect to any symptoms that may require diagnosis or medical attention.

The views expressed are those of the author and should not be taken as expert instruction or commands. The reader is responsible for his or her own actions.

Adherence to all applicable laws and regulations, including international, federal, state, and local governing professional licensing, business practices, advertising, and all other aspects of doing business in the US, Canada, or any other jurisdiction is the sole responsibility of the reader.

The author does not assume any responsibility or liability whatsoever on the behalf of the reader of this material.

Book formatting and cover design: www.bookclaw.com
Editor: Sana Abuleil
Photo credits: Flawless j photography

Books may be purchased in quantity and for special sales by contacting Kala Jordan-Lindsey at: **Write@kalajordanlindsey.com**

For more information, please contact:
Kala Jordan-Lindsey
Write@kalajordanlindsey.com
www.kalajordanlindsey.com

To book a consultation, email:
Write@kalajordanlindsey.com

To **you**

Table of Contents

Introduction 6

How to Get the Most Out of this Book 7

Inspirational and Motivational Quotations to Strengthen Your Mental, Physical, and Spiritual Health 8

Acknowledgements 353

Other Books by Kala Jordan-Lindsey 354

The Most Powerful Quotes to Enhance Your Life

Introduction

Quotations are powerful, and can completely transform your day or your mindset. Something as simple as a word of encouragement from a friend or loved one holds so much influence. If you're down, expect to be uplifted, and if you're unmotivated, expect to be motivated. Inspirational quotations also offer wisdom and insight to enlighten you with a seed of hope. Especially in difficult times. Quotations enhance your mental, physical, and spiritual health offering an eye-opening experience from a different vantage point. Quotations are therapeutic and promote positivity. They're also effective and fun for everyday reading, which allows you to connect with each message on a deeper level.

Some of these quotations are meant to make you laugh, some are meant to inspire you, some are meant to make you cry, and some are even meant to calm your heart. But all these quotations are meant to encourage you in your everyday life—one day at a time.

So, take your time and embrace this appetizer. Let this book inspire you to live on purpose, to live life to the fullest, to smile and love more, and to welcome more positivity, joy, peace, and happiness into your life. It's the perfect book to help you along your life journey. It's short, sweet, and worth the reading experience!

Cheers to you and your loved ones.

Thank you,

Kala Jordan-Lindsey

Table of Contents

Introduction 6

How to Get the Most Out of this Book 7

Inspirational and Motivational Quotations to Strengthen Your Mental, Physical, and Spiritual Health 8

Acknowledgements 353

Other Books by Kala Jordan-Lindsey 354

The Most Powerful Quotes to Enhance Your Life

Introduction

Quotations are powerful, and can completely transform your day or your mindset. Something as simple as a word of encouragement from a friend or loved one holds so much influence. If you're down, expect to be uplifted, and if you're unmotivated, expect to be motivated. Inspirational quotations also offer wisdom and insight to enlighten you with a seed of hope. Especially in difficult times. Quotations enhance your mental, physical, and spiritual health offering an eye-opening experience from a different vantage point. Quotations are therapeutic and promote positivity. They're also effective and fun for everyday reading, which allows you to connect with each message on a deeper level.

Some of these quotations are meant to make you laugh, some are meant to inspire you, some are meant to make you cry, and some are even meant to calm your heart. But all these quotations are meant to encourage you in your everyday life—one day at a time.

So, take your time and embrace this appetizer. Let this book inspire you to live on purpose, to live life to the fullest, to smile and love more, and to welcome more positivity, joy, peace, and happiness into your life. It's the perfect book to help you along your life journey. It's short, sweet, and worth the reading experience!

Cheers to you and your loved ones.

Thank you,

Kala Jordan-Lindsey

How to Get the Most Out of this Book

This book has been created to work in several ways:

1. It's an unlimited day journey that you can start at any time, but consistency is important. Read one quotation a day, and allow that quotation to encourage you for the entire day. Write it down, carry it with you, and read it often as needed. Take a few minutes and write down any thoughts or feelings you have about it. You will be amazed at the immediate impact you will experience with this process.

2. You may read this book like any book by letting it do the following: inhale and exhale after meditating on a quotation or two. Let it resonate in your mind as you reflect on its positive meaning. Taste it as you embrace the physical experience, and have a moment of silence as you reflect on the quotation(s).

3. You may choose a quotation and journal about how it applies to your life, or go the extra mile and write a book about it. Choose from over a hundred topics!

4. You can create a vision board as a reference for encouragement, or place each quotation in a glass jar or shoe box so you can pick one out each day to meditate on and embrace.

5. Have fun and enjoy this book! Share it with family, friends, and loved ones, and even strangers—you'll never know whose life you'll touch by doing something small, but big in God's eyes.

Inspirational and Motivational Quotations to Strengthen Your Mental, Physical, and Spiritual Health

Love like today was your last because tomorrow is not promised.

-Kala Jordan-Lindsey

If you welcome positivity into your life, you'll strengthen your health. You'll be happier and healthier.

-Kala Jordan-Lindsey

God has the power to create something amazing from your imperfections and struggles in life if you believe it.

-Kala Jordan-Lindsey

Do something with your life so that it doesn't go to waste where others bury their stories.

-Kala Jordan-Lindsey

A dose of wisdom to your schedule won't hurt. It'll help your day go by smoother.

-Kala Jordan-Lindsey

Look in the mirror. You're beautiful and blessed.

-Kala Jordan-Lindsey

You're stronger than your most significant failure.

-Kala Jordan-Lindsey

The Most Powerful Quotes to Enhance Your Life

Your heart is precious, so embrace every heartbeat on purpose.

-Kala Jordan-Lindsey

It's time to be optimistic, and it starts now.

-Kala Jordan-Lindsey

Your heart lights up the world like the Son.

-Kala Jordan-Lindsey

Be the change because change starts with you.

-Kala Jordan-Lindsey

It's okay to be encouraged by wisdom if what you're doing in life isn't working.

-Kala Jordan-Lindsey

You were created to rise like the sun—to stand like a soldier, immovable and determined, when life gets difficult.

-Kala Jordan-Lindsey

Just because everybody does what they want to do doesn't mean you have to do what everybody else does.

-Kala Jordan-Lindsey

Be happy the moment you open your eyes.

-Kala Jordan-Lindsey

Life is about learning from your past mistakes so that you can make better choices today and in the future.

-Kala Jordan-Lindsey

Believe in yourself, but have faith in the Creator, first.

-Kala Jordan-Lindsey

Your heart is powerful like a contagious virus.

-Kala Jordan-Lindsey

Problems are difficult if you're trying to figure them out. Let God solve them.

-Kala Jordan-Lindsey

Like me but follow Jesus.

-Kala Jordan-Lindsey

Give up your GPS to follow Christ, who leads to true life.

-Kala Jordan-Lindsey

If you're down, lift your head. If you're anxious, be still and pray. And if you're uncertain, have faith.

—Kala Jordan-Lindsey

Express yourself like a colorful painting.

—Kala Jordan-Lindsey

Let your creativity and passion be seen like a beautiful painting on the wall.

—Kala Jordan-Lindsey

Your problems are not as big as you think for God to rescue you.

-Kala Jordan-Lindsey

There's power in your pain, so keep your head up.

-Kala Jordan-Lindsey

Your past testifies about the goodness of God, about the realness of His grace and mercy in your life.

-Kala Jordan-Lindsey

Let your why to be more significant than your what.

-Kala Jordan-Lindsey

Your faith is stronger when you're certain that God is making no mistakes in your life.

-Kala Jordan-Lindsey

Reading a good book releases negative vibes and relaxes your mind.

-Kala Jordan-Lindsey

Laughter creates hope in others that are hopeless and depressed.

    -Kala Jordan-Lindsey

The best memories you can create are the ones today.

    -Kala Jordan-Lindsey

Your experiences should make you stronger each time without a doubt.

    -Kala Jordan-Lindsey

Living in the past can depress you or weaken your mind if you stay there and never move.

-Kala Jordan-Lindsey

There's joy in your storms if you know who's greater than your unexpectedness in life.

-Kala Jordan-Lindsey

God will bless you with the skills and knowledge you need to overcome life. So, don't worry. Stay prayerful in your moments of worry and anxiety.

-Kala Jordan-Lindsey

Allowing drama into your life is unhealthy and will drain you if you let it.

-Kala Jordan-Lindsey

The road is dim and difficult without Jesus.

-Kala Jordan-Lindsey

Rise and speak out, or someone else will.

-Kala Jordan-Lindsey

A person with a strong mindset has the power to overcome the unexpected roadblocks of life.

-Kala Jordan-Lindsey

You're stronger and wiser than your past, so embrace today.

-Kala Jordan-Lindsey

When you walk through the valley of health issues or financial difficulties, don't lose your mind. Be still and exercise your faith.

-Kala Jordan-Lindsey

You're not dumb; you were created with common sense. So, embrace your intelligence.

-Kala Jordan-Lindsey

Don't waste your gift; share it with the world instead.

-Kala Jordan-Lindsey

Your time on earth is limited, so give it all that you have. Empty what you were designed to release before taking your final breath.

-Kala Jordan-Lindsey

Your future is bright, so think positive and shine your light before it dims.

-Kala Jordan-Lindsey

Eating a fresh orange in the morning is healthier than complaining about your life.

-Kala Jordan-Lindsey

God will elevate you amid a storm, so trust His will.

-Kala Jordan-Lindsey

You're full of creativity and brilliant ideas. Share it all with others.

-Kala Jordan-Lindsey

I'm touched to know you were touched.

-Kala Jordan-Lindsey

Bless others and God will forever bless you with favor.

-Kala Jordan-Lindsey

Adding garlic to your foods has more impact than pouring hot sauce over a bowl of collard greens.

-Kala Jordan-Lindsey

Medicine has the power to heal you, but positive words have the power to inspire and comfort a weak heart.

-Kala Jordan-Lindsey

Bless your husband with what he loves, and he'll love you for it; give him love.

-Kala Jordan-Lindsey

You may lose weight if you spend more time exercising than at the bar.

-Kala Jordan-Lindsey

If you don't know where to release your thoughts and feelings, unclog them on paper.

-Kala Jordan-Lindsey

Share yesterday's story but live for today with hope for tomorrow.

-Kala Jordan-Lindsey

If you have nothing written on the page, you're wasting your time and talents. You were born to share your stories. Don't hold back; release your experiences to the world to help others in their difficult moments of life.

-Kala Jordan-Lindsey

Cotton candy is sweet, but dark chocolate is heathier for your body.

-Kala Jordan-Lindsey

Don't follow me, follow Jesus.

-Kala Jordan-Lindsey

Try praying more than you gossip and you'll have better relationships with others.

-Kala Jordan-Lindsey

Appreciating life is when you desire to make the best of uncontrollable and messy situations.

-Kala Jordan-Lindsey

True happiness is temporary if it's not embraced in Jesus Christ.

-Kala Jordan-Lindsey

Be happy and smile because you're living. There are millions in the grave who aren't. You're blessed.

-Kala Jordan-Lindsey

Relax and take a breather. Everything will be okay.

-Kala Jordan-Lindsey

If you're drained, don't wear yourself out. Go on a nice vacation, put your phone on vibrate, and have a glass of water in the sun.

-Kala Jordan-Lindsey

You're human, so expect to make mistakes.

-Kala Jordan-Lindsey

Don't worry about being perfect. There's only One who is—God, our Heavenly Father.

-Kala Jordan-Lindsey

Pray and persevere when you find yourself in the eye of a storm. You'll overcome it like the one you overcame yesterday.

-Kala Jordan-Lindsey

God is the publisher. He owns the copyrights to your life.

-Kala Jordan-Lindsey

Drinking a glass of water with lemon is healthier than going to bed angry and on an empty stomach.

-Kala Jordan-Lindsey

Take care of yourself or you'll waste your precious life away.

-Kala Jordan-Lindsey

You're free to scribble on the page because your story won't be perfect.

-Kala Jordan-Lindsey

Life is difficult unless you have faith to realize there's hope in this dark world.

-Kala Jordan-Lindsey

Achieving a goal takes time and can be difficult. But the process is satisfying. So, if you're striving and struggling, never give up. It's a part of life, like experiencing a storm. We all wrestle before we win. Pray and be patient.

-Kala Jordan-Lindsey

Focus on building positive relationships rather than tearing others down with negativity.

-Kala Jordan-Lindsey

A person carrying a negative attitude is unhappy. If your attitude stinks, surround yourself with positive-minded people and you'll smell better.

-Kala Jordan-Lindsey

Be happy because tomorrow isn't guaranteed.

-Kala Jordan-Lindsey

Surround yourself with good-hearted company and you'll be happier.

-Kala Jordan-Lindsey

You have over a thousand reasons to never give up; so, keep going and never give up.

-Kala Jordan-Lindsey

Joy can't be bought because it's a gift from God.

-Kala Jordan-Lindsey

Enjoy the present and stop walking in the past.

-Kala Jordan-Lindsey

Learn to share and use your gift for others.

-Kala Jordan-Lindsey

When you're at your lowest moments and doubtful no one is listening, have faith because God hears you.

-Kala Jordan-Lindsey

Don't sweat what's out of your control; give it all to God.

-Kala Jordan-Lindsey

Exercise until you sweat because burning calories is a blessing.

-Kala Jordan-Lindsey

Be determined to remove unnecessary trash from your life, or you'll continue to be distracted.

-Kala Jordan-Lindsey

True happiness is being thankful and content. It's appreciating life when you're up and when you're down. It's having a loving and joyful heart in the Lord.

-Kala Jordan-Lindsey

Be happy, or be miserable. The choice is yours.

-Kala Jordan-Lindsey

Let your creativity shine and others will release theirs.

-Kala Jordan-Lindsey

You're stronger than your illness, so, be encouraged to wait on the Lord for your deliverance.

-Kala Jordan-Lindsey

Be the light in someone's darkness because you are.

-Kala Jordan-Lindsey

Those with a noisy heart should be still and pray for God's peace.

-Kala Jordan-Lindsey

It's hard to breathe when you worship idols, so humble yourself and reverence the Lord.

-Kala Jordan-Lindsey

Start today if you're ready to experience a new chapter in your life.

-Kala Jordan-Lindsey

Couples in an unhealthy marriage have the potential to overcome and rectify their issues with the power and strength of the Almighty.

-Kala Jordan-Lindsey

Elevation is powered by the grace of God.

-Kala Jordan-Lindsey

Let the noise of life inspire you to stay focused on your heavenly prize.

-Kala Jordan-Lindsey

When you live in the Lord, you're living rather than just rotating with the earth.

-Kala Jordan-Lindsey

Stand strong and immovable like a tree amid a storm.

-Kala Jordan-Lindsey

Wherever you are, encourage someone to never give up.

-Kala Jordan-Lindsey

Blossom in your calling like a flower.

-Kala Jordan-Lindsey

When God opens your eyes, He'll do it like curtains being drawn—slowly and gradually.

-Kala Jordan-Lindsey

When you have the favor of God in your life, adding flavor to your life is not necessary.

-Kala Jordan-Lindsey

You're almost there, so keep going.

-Kala Jordan-Lindsey

Bless someone by giving them positive advice and encouragement.

-Kala Jordan-Lindsey

You rock the world, baby.

-Kala Jordan-Lindsey

You're not a writer; you're a human being who loves to release your heart.

-Kala Jordan-Lindsey

Don't be cold. Be nice.

-Kala Jordan-Lindsey

If you roll with Jesus, He'll stick by your side.

-Kala Jordan-Lindsey

Save and invest if you want to enjoy retirement.

-Kala Jordan-Lindsey

Your darkest moment is always someone's best day ever.

-Kala Jordan-Lindsey

Your likes don't count. Count your blessings.

-Kala Jordan-Lindsey

Determination is when you see the blessing on the other side. So, never let anyone distract you from achieving your goals in life.

-Kala Jordan-Lindsey

Fill your space with creativity, and smile.

-Kala Jordan-Lindsey

Dance with a smile because you know it'll improve your health and inspire others to do the same.

-Kala Jordan-Lindsey

Cherish your relationship with the Lord compared to nothing else in the world.

-Kala Jordan-Lindsey

It's easy to make friends, but it's hard to keep them. Make friends anyway.

-Kala Jordan-Lindsey

Embrace your health or it'll fail you like a car with a bad engine.

-Kala Jordan-Lindsey

True happiness comes from God.

-Kala Jordan-Lindsey

Put the broom down; only God can clean up your life.

-Kala Jordan-Lindsey

When you stop seeking the Lord, life will have you on the search like the FBI.

-Kala Jordan-Lindsey

Be brave when life tests you.

-Kala Jordan-Lindsey

Don't worry; you'll pass the test if you believe it deep down in your soul.

-Kala Jordan-Lindsey

Stay focused so you're not distracted by nonsense.

-Kala Jordan-Lindsey

You're special just the way you are.

-Kala Jordan-Lindsey

When you face challenges in life, give it your best and never give up.

-Kala Jordan-Lindsey

Jesus adds flavor to your life unlike hot peppers.

-Kala Jordan-Lindsey

When God reveals your calling, run towards it and perform, or else you'll miss your stop.

-Kala Jordan-Lindsey

If you feel like expressing yourself, sing on the page.

-Kala Jordan-Lindsey

There's hope in Hope, our Lord and Savior.

-Kala Jordan-Lindsey

Wherever you are on the mountain, keep climbing and never give up.

-Kala Jordan-Lindsey

A human-being without purpose is lifeless. And life without purpose is worthless.

-Kala Jordan-Lindsey

Embrace the Word; He's real.

-Kala Jordan-Lindsey

God keeps our eyes open and our heart beating.

-Kala Jordan-Lindsey

The most important power you'll ever need is from God, our Heavenly Father.

-Kala Jordan-Lindsey

An elevator can only take you so high, but God has the power to elevate you beyond your imagination.

-Kala Jordan-Lindsey

If you connect with Jesus, He'll connect with you.

-Kala Jordan-Lindsey

If you roll with Jesus; He'll never leave your side.

—Kala Jordan-Lindsey

Invite positivity in your home and remove negativity. Reminder: one negative-minded person will poison the whole party.

—Kala Jordan-Lindsey

Worshipping idols will cause your life to end before your destined number.

—Kala Jordan-Lindsey

If you pursue God's purpose, you'll discover your own.

-Kala Jordan-Lindsey

If you're restless, talk to Jesus.

-Kala Jordan-Lindsey

The power of God can restore a broken heart.

-Kala Jordan-Lindsey

Take your time with everything you do in life, or you'll suffer with anxiety and panic attacks.

-Kala Jordan-Lindsey

I love to write like a rapper; listen to my story.

-Kala Jordan-Lindsey

Don't forget your life. Spend more time improving your mental, physical, and spiritual health.

-Kala Jordan-Lindsey

Get out of your head and let God open your eyes.

-Kala Jordan-Lindsey

Hard work will always pay off if you stay focused and thankful.

-Kala Jordan-Lindsey

If you're married, burn more calories by having more sex.

-Kala Jordan-Lindsey

If you have asthma, it's common sense not to smoke. Take better care of your health before something serious happens.

-Kala Jordan-Lindsey

Replace violence with a pen and pad; release your feelings on the page because it's more powerful than a dangerous instrument.

-Kala Jordan-Lindsey

Something as simple as preparing your husband's lunch for work has the biggest impact, and he'll love you for it.

-Kala Jordan-Lindsey

Disconnect with the world because your mind is all over the place.

-Kala Jordan-Lindsey

Love what you're called to do in life, or else you'll be miserable, unsatisfied, and unfulfilled.

-Kala Jordan-Lindsey

If you're unemployed, put your gifts to use and God will bless you to make at least a dollar. Just never give up along the way.

-Kala Jordan-Lindsey

You have no reason to get off track if you keep your eyes on Jesus.

-Kala Jordan-Lindsey

Wherever you are in life, keep striving and never quit.

-Kala Jordan-Lindsey

Focus on Jesus in your struggles; you'll see Him through your mess.

-Kala Jordan-Lindsey

Something as simple as saying, "Thank you" has the power to do the unimaginable.

-Kala Jordan-Lindsey

Positive vibes are allowed; drama is not permitted.

-Kala Jordan-Lindsey

Every time you struggle, know that God is squeezing the dark out of you so you can glorify Him and release your purpose.

-Kala Jordan-Lindsey

You can't finish unless you start, so what are you waiting for? Go!

-Kala Jordan-Lindsey

One of the most difficult things about writing a book is delivering what many are struggling with today. So, keep pushing and deliver your story. It will resonate with someone.

-Kala Jordan-Lindsey

It doesn't matter if you're at the bottom; in Christ, you'll always be at the top.

-Kala Jordan-Lindsey

If you're jobless, embrace the gifts God created you with and watch how He turns your life around.

-Kala Jordan-Lindsey

When you allow God to take over your breath, your mental and physical health will improve.

-Kala Jordan-Lindsey

Keep your faith unless you want to be imprisoned in darkness for the rest of your life.
  -Kala Jordan-Lindsey

If you panic, stop, and pray. Then, read a Bible verse and know that God will calm your heart.

-Kala Jordan-Lindsey

God will calm your anxious heart if you seek Him first.

-Kala Jordan-Lindsey

You are not a mistake; you were created by an awesome God, the Greatest Designer in the universe.

-Kala Jordan-Lindsey

If you want to write a book, go for it. You can do it, but know that God will make it happen.

-Kala Jordan-Lindsey

Don't ever give up at a dead end. If you're there, look for Jesus to give you direction. He'll guide you safely to where you need to be.

-Kala Jordan-Lindsey

God blessed you with strength to overcome the storm, so, be bold and courageous as He delivers you to shore.

-Kala Jordan-Lindsey

God will never give you a test that you can't pass because He's the Creator and He is fair and just.

-Kala Jordan-Lindsey

Obstacles are designed to strengthen your hope, faith, and love in the Lord.

-Kala Jordan-Lindsey

You're not crazy; you're human.

-Kala Jordan-Lindsey

Look for the rainbow after the storm.

-Kala Jordan-Lindsey

Jesus always calms the storm when it seems to be the most chaotic.

-Kala Jordan-Lindsey

You stand out like the stars in the sky.

-Kala Jordan-Lindsey

Having a relationship with Christ is the best relationship ever. You'll never crave for another.

-Kala Jordan-Lindsey

If you're bored, get up and do something with your precious life.

-Kala Jordan-Lindsey

Stand like a tree and be fearless.

-Kala Jordan-Lindsey

There's a lot to be thankful for when you hit rock bottom.

-Kala Jordan-Lindsey

I admire your incredible resilience.

-Kala Jordan-Lindsey

Let the volume of Jesus be louder than the volume of the rest of the world.

-Kala Jordan-Lindsey

You have over a thousand reasons why you're living. Make it count.

-Kala Jordan-Lindsey

You're stronger than the situation, and God is greater than the outcome.

-Kala Jordan-Lindsey

It's better to chase Jesus than to be chased by the cops.

-Kala Jordan-Lindsey

If you want your health to improve, include Jesus in your diet.

-Kala Jordan-Lindsey

The best recipes are made with faith.

-Kala Jordan-Lindsey

God will never leave you, but man will.

-Kala Jordan-Lindsey

You're human, so you'll never have a perfect story. So, have confidence about sharing your struggles in life.

-Kala Jordan-Lindsey

You're a blessing because you inspire others to live happy and healthier lives.

-Kala Jordan-Lindsey

A life without Jesus is like a blind man roaming the earth without purpose.

-Kala Jordan-Lindsey

Jesus is the most powerful call center. He's always available.

-Kala Jordan-Lindsey

Don't rely on anybody but God. He is the only One who will never let you down.

-Kala Jordan-Lindsey

Faith is seeing the victory before it happens.

-Kala Jordan-Lindsey

God loves you more than the person in the mirror.

-Kala Jordan-Lindsey

God's blessings have nothing to do with your zip code, but have everything to do with your relationship in Him.

-Kala Jordan-Lindsey

If I told you where I resided, you'd be surprised, but if I told you who resides in me, you'd be touched.

-Kala Jordan-Lindsey

Praise God all day, every day, and never stop.

-Kala Jordan-Lindsey

Dieting and exercising aren't enough. We need Jesus.

-Kala Jordan-Lindsey

Pray for God's plans and you'll release yours in due time.

-Kala Jordan-Lindsey

Never give up in the middle of the fight. With God, you'll win.

-Kala Jordan-Lindsey

You're strong, so rise and keep climbing.

-Kala Jordan-Lindsey

One of the greatest desires of human beings is not only to live a "successful" life, but also to express.

-Kala Jordan-Lindsey

Take your time in bed; make love.

-Kala Jordan-Lindsey

If you desire love, joy, peace, and happiness over money, you'll be blessed with money, too.

-Kala Jordan-Lindsey

Your hands tell me more about your life than your neighborhood.

-Kala Jordan-Lindsey

Your heart speaks louder than your zip code.

-Kala Jordan-Lindsey

Your greatest fear will change your life.

-Kala Jordan-Lindsey

Embrace your body or else it'll fail you.

-Kala Jordan-Lindsey

You are never too old to overcome life. You're built to experience victory until your last breath on earth.

-Kala Jordan-Lindsey

Go for a walk and embrace the fresh air.

-Kala Jordan-Lindsey

Write without thinking and you'll be successful.

-Kala Jordan-Lindsey

Thirty minutes of burning calories a day is more powerful than grinding each day without success.

-Kala Jordan-Lindsey

When you choose not to be distracted by noise or drama, you learn to appreciate the peace and quiet God gives you.

-Kala Jordan-Lindsey

You're a special hero.

-Kala Jordan-Lindsey

Be creative on paper; express from the heart.

-Kala Jordan-Lindsey

Uncomfortable situations in life make you stronger, so, embrace them with faith.

-Kala Jordan-Lindsey

Pressure will always test your faith.

-Kala Jordan-Lindsey

Embrace your pain because somebody will be inspired by your strength.

-Kala Jordan-Lindsey

God is doing something amazing in your life, so, trust the process.

-Kala Jordan-Lindsey

Embrace His grace while you're receiving it.

-Kala Jordan-Lindsey

If you want to live a fulfilled life, do everything possible to listen and follow Jesus.

-Kala Jordan-Lindsey

Keep your eyes on the One; He is most important.

-Kala Jordan-Lindsey

The person who follows the crowd lacks confidence and self-esteem to lead.

-Kala Jordan-Lindsey

A leader is humble and sets a positive example.

-Kala Jordan-Lindsey

Lead with unwavering faith and joy.

-Kala Jordan-Lindsey

There's nobody like daddy.

-Kala Jordan-Lindsey

Sometimes, God has to tweak your life for improvements to occur.

-Kala Jordan-Lindsey

Let God's word guide you through the storm.

-Kala Jordan-Lindsey

The mistakes you made before you came to Christ weren't you, so, it's okay. Don't look down on yourself; you're still worthy and a beautiful jewel.

-Kala Jordan-Lindsey

The Most Powerful Quotes to Enhance Your Life

Live one day at a time; don't get ahead of the process. Be patient and wait.

-Kala Jordan-Lindsey

Time is running out; do something with your precious life.

-Kala Jordan-Lindsey

When it's dark, turn on your light.

-Kala Jordan-Lindsey

If you have to fight, fight with the word of God as your weapon.

-Kala Jordan-Lindsey

The very story you don't want to share with the world is the one that will inspire your neighbor to never give up.

-Kala Jordan-Lindsey

If you open up to God, others will be touched by your life and desire to follow Him.

-Kala Jordan-Lindsey

The good part about writing a book is that you get to release what has the power to uplift others.

-Kala Jordan-Lindsey

Writing is more powerful than giving up.

-Kala Jordan-Lindsey

Writing a book is serious business. It'll touch your life and help inspire another. Go for it; start writing.

-Kala Jordan-Lindsey

When you shed tears while writing a book, know that you have a best seller. So, always write from the heart with confidence in your story.

-Kala Jordan-Lindsey

Sometimes God has to clean up your house to make room for the other blessings He has in store for you.

-Kala Jordan-Lindsey

Your story has the power to ripple out into the world, touching more lives than you can count. Write.

-Kala Jordan-Lindsey

Authentic power comes from God.

-Kala Jordan-Lindsey

If you have a loving, respectful, God-sent husband, keep him.

-Kala Jordan-Lindsey

If your husband sends you messages that give you butterflies and goosebumps, return your love.

-Kala Jordan-Lindsey

One of the greatest joys in life is having an amazing and loving spouse who loves to cook, clean, and wash clothes.

-Kala Jordan-Lindsey

One of the greatest blessings is to be in love with a man who loves you for you.

-Kala Jordan-Lindsey

If your husband texts you three hearts, text him five hearts; give him more love.

-Kala Jordan-Lindsey

Sometimes God will snatch you out of situations so He can save your life. So, when He does, be thankful because it could have been you.

-Kala Jordan-Lindsey

Sometimes God will use your imperfections, flaws, and blemishes so that others can glorify His name.

-Kala Jordan-Lindsey

You can do it, but God will make it happen.

-Kala Jordan-Lindsey

Sometimes God will take you through a storm to remove clutter and burdens from your life.

-Kala Jordan-Lindsey

Your biggest failure will be your greatest blessing for the world. So, the more you fail, embrace the will of God. There's a reason why it's happening.

-Kala Jordan-Lindsey

If you're writing a book, write out loud; be bold and release your passion. Stay true to your calling.

-Kala Jordan-Lindsey

Writing a book empowers you to share everything you ever desired to release, and even the things you never thought you'd share.

-Kala Jordan-Lindsey

Your imperfections touch lives. Own them.

-Kala Jordan-Lindsey

Your voice is loud, so sing.

-Kala Jordan-Lindsey

When God reveals your life calling, life gets better.

-Kala Jordan-Lindsey

When you seek God, you'll find the One you needed all the while long. So, be patient.

-Kala Jordan-Lindsey

God sometimes speaks to man in a storm, so embrace His voice.

-Kala Jordan-Lindsey

The Most Powerful Quotes to Enhance Your Life

Gain a relationship with Christ before you invest in one from the world.

-Kala Jordan-Lindsey

There is peace in my home as it is in my heart.

-Kala Jordan-Lindsey

Everything you're doing today will pay off tomorrow.

-Kala Jordan-Lindsey

Let God be the conductor of your life.

-Kala Jordan-Lindsey

You're almost there, so keep going and never give up.

-Kala Jordan-Lindsey

Don't make it complicated. Keep things simple and move on.

-Kala Jordan-Lindsey

Focus on the positive things of life, not the negative.

-Kala Jordan-Lindsey

You can't function if you're mentally, physically, and spiritually ill. So, focus on becoming holistically healthy so you can excel.

-Kala Jordan-Lindsey

If you worship doubt, then you'll always be sick.

-Kala Jordan-Lindsey

Write because your story matters. Be bold and release it unapologetically. You're almost there, so keep going and faith it out.

-Kala Jordan-Lindsey

If you want something bad enough in life, you'll go get it.

-Kala Jordan-Lindsey

To seek Jesus is beyond discovering a jewel; it's bigger and more powerful.

-Kala Jordan-Lindsey

Mountains are difficult to climb if you're mentally, physically, and spiritually weak.

-Kala Jordan-Lindsey

Just because you failed doesn't mean you'll never win. You were born to win through your failures.

-Kala Jordan-Lindsey

A simple text makes his day.

-Kala Jordan-Lindsey

God blessed you with everything you need to execute your calling. Use it. Don't abuse it.

-Kala Jordan-Lindsey

You're restless because your heart is troubled.

-Kala Jordan-Lindsey

Failures are designed to encourage you to rise and reach higher—to strive and never give up in life.

-Kala Jordan-Lindsey

Be brave enough to love yourself more than ever.

-Kala Jordan-Lindsey

Doing anything in life without purpose is like a blind man walking in the middle of traffic.

-Kala Jordan-Lindsey

Take a breather to clear your mind.

-Kala Jordan-Lindsey

A heart that's noisy needs to be uplifted.

-Kala Jordan-Lindsey

Your bestselling book is hidden in your heart; deliver it.

-Kala Jordan-Lindsey

You're struggling with life because God is trying to get your undivided attention.

-Kala Jordan-Lindsey

Stop and turn to God before your time is up.

-Kala Jordan-Lindsey

Let God help you with your problems.

-Kala Jordan-Lindsey

It's easy to become distracted in life when you're not focused, so, stay focused.

-Kala Jordan-Lindsey

The moment you take your eyes off God, you begin to struggle with life.

-Kala Jordan-Lindsey

The Most Powerful Quotes to Enhance Your Life

Be inspired when you look in the mirror.

-Kala Jordan-Lindsey

You're stronger than you were yesterday, and weaker than you will be tomorrow.

-Kala Jordan-Lindsey

Facing adversity will make you stronger and wiser in the end.

-Kala Jordan-Lindsey

The Most Powerful Quotes to Enhance Your Life

There's perfection in God, but not man.

-Kala Jordan-Lindsey

You're enough; don't edit your appearance.

-Kala Jordan-Lindsey

God can change your identity, but not your appearance. Be grateful for all He's given you.

-Kala Jordan-Lindsey

There's always hope to be better, stronger, and wiser than yesterday by the power of grace.

-Kala Jordan-Lindsey

Expect a miracle to happen.

-Kala Jordan-Lindsey

Expect great things to happen in your life and they will.

-Kala Jordan-Lindsey

Be stronger than your storms.

-Kala Jordan-Lindsey

Wisdom will strengthen your spiritual growth.

-Kala Jordan-Lindsey

Never give up on your goals even if you have to start from square one.

-Kala Jordan-Lindsey

You look like how you feel because you need help as we all do.

-Kala Jordan-Lindsey

By the grace of God, you will succeed no matter how difficult life gets.

-Kala Jordan-Lindsey

The more you struggle with life, the closer God is pushing you where you need to be.

-Kala Jordan-Lindsey

You're worth more than your wildest dreams.

-Kala Jordan-Lindsey

Dreams can become a reality if your calling is your reality.

-Kala Jordan-Lindsey

Get out of your feelings and chill.

-Kala Jordan-Lindsey

Get up and keep moving. You have a race to win.

-Kala Jordan-Lindsey

You're beautiful when you're authentic; keep it real.

-Kala Jordan-Lindsey

God will help you create something special out of your struggles in life. Believe it and embrace the process.

-Kala Jordan-Lindsey

*You're stronger than you think.
Believe it and go for it.*

-Kala Jordan-Lindsey

*God's word has the power to
uplift a broken heart.*

-Kala Jordan-Lindsey

*You were created to be successful,
so keep striving.*

-Kala Jordan-Lindsey

You'll make it to the top if you climb with Jesus.

-Kala Jordan-Lindsey

Your beautiful smile melts my heart.

-Kala Jordan-Lindsey

Get closer to God while you can.

-Kala Jordan-Lindsey

The Most Powerful Quotes to Enhance Your Life

Inhale and exhale if you feel anxious.

-Kala Jordan-Lindsey

God will uplift you when you're humble.

-Kala Jordan-Lindsey

Pray before you gossip with friends.

-Kala Jordan-Lindsey

Run to Jesus before you run to man.

-Kala Jordan-Lindsey

Your positive attitude lights up the entire globe.

-Kala Jordan-Lindsey

Love deeper than the depths of the oceans.

-Kala Jordan-Lindsey

The Most Powerful Quotes to Enhance Your Life

Don't be afraid to sweat. It's worth every drip.

-Kala Jordan-Lindsey

You weren't born to sit; move your body.

-Kala Jordan-Lindsey

Dance your calories away. Go for it and have fun!

-Kala Jordan-Lindsey

You're in shape, so exercise.

-Kala Jordan-Lindsey

You're almost there so keep going.

-Kala Jordan-Lindsey

Stand still and pray if your heart is noisy.

-Kala Jordan-Lindsey

You're more powerful than you think.

-Kala Jordan-Lindsey

God blessed you to shine like a diamond.

-Kala Jordan-Lindsey

Your calling is deeper than a dream. It's revealed to you in Christ.

-Kala Jordan-Lindsey

Life gets better when you embrace your faith.

-Kala Jordan-Lindsey

When you become anxious, pray and be confident that every little thing will be alright.

-Kala Jordan-Lindsey

Your mind is somewhere else. Stay focused.

-Kala Jordan-Lindsey

The Most Powerful Quotes to Enhance Your Life

Your heart is one of a kind; you have no match.

-Kala Jordan-Lindsey

Your signature is special.

-Kala Jordan-Lindsey

Sing your heart out with confidence.

-Kala Jordan-Lindsey

I love you from the heart.

-Kala Jordan-Lindsey

Embrace whatever God reveals to you.

-Kala Jordan-Lindsey

God is preparing you to experience a turning point.

-Kala Jordan-Lindsey

God gives the best raises, so turn to Him.

-Kala Jordan-Lindsey

Focus on positive things in life like helping others overcome challenges.

-Kala Jordan-Lindsey

Embrace your power; you won't always have it.

-Kala Jordan-Lindsey

Promote positivity. Kind words comfort others.

-Kala Jordan-Lindsey

There's always a bigger picture in God's plan. He'll eventually reveal it to you. Be patient and don't rush the process.

-Kala Jordan-Lindsey

God's plan will bless you where you need to be.

-Kala Jordan-Lindsey

You stand out like the colors in the rainbow, but you shine brighter than them all.

-Kala Jordan-Lindsey

You're bright like yellow.

-Kala Jordan-Lindsey

God is preparing to take you higher than your imagination. Believe it.

-Kala Jordan-Lindsey

Embracing your failures is where growth begins.

-Kala Jordan-Lindsey

Without faith, it's difficult to overcome life. Exercise your confidence, and you'll succeed.

-Kala Jordan-Lindsey

You're stronger than your battles, but God is greater.

-Kala Jordan-Lindsey

You don't need an umbrella. In Jesus, you're covered.

-Kala Jordan-Lindsey

God is more powerful than your greatest issues.

-Kala Jordan-Lindsey

Let gratitude take over your life.

-Kala Jordan-Lindsey

Be bold and courageous for a greater purpose.

-Kala Jordan-Lindsey

Hope is alive; spread it.

-Kala Jordan-Lindsey

Be sassy and confident when you walk on stage.

-Kala Jordan-Lindsey

Your greatest fear may be your life calling. So, face your fears with faith.

-Kala Jordan-Lindsey

You touch lives when you release your gift and passion.

-Kala Jordan-Lindsey

You're blessed with favor by an awesome God.

-Kala Jordan-Lindsey

You add flavor to the table.

-Kala Jordan-Lindsey

You're blessed with hands that have the power to inspire lives and open eyes.

-Kala Jordan-Lindsey

What you discover in God will always be more valuable than silver and gold.

-Kala Jordan-Lindsey

Every day is a process worth embracing. Trust the process and never give up.

-Kala Jordan-Lindsey

Leaving the past behind is harder than moving forward because your mind is playing tricks on you. Get out of your head and move forward one day at a time.

-Kala Jordan-Lindsey

God is taking you somewhere, so be prepared.

-Kala Jordan-Lindsey

The Most Powerful Quotes to Enhance Your Life

You don't need to roll an 8-ball to discover your purpose; God will reveal it to you by faith.

-Kala Jordan-Lindsey

God is with you; listen to your heartbeat.

-Kala Jordan-Lindsey

Never give up; you're almost at the finish line.

-Kala Jordan-Lindsey

God will reveal the bigger picture of your storms in life. You will find joy and peace in what He reveals. Appreciate it.

-Kala Jordan-Lindsey

Embrace the joy and peace in your storms of life.

-Kala Jordan-Lindsey

You're beautiful like a garden, so smile.

-Kala Jordan-Lindsey

Take joy in your struggles; unexpectedness is designed to strengthen you.

-Kala Jordan-Lindsey

Your spiritual status is more important than your social status—that's a fact.

-Kala Jordan-Lindsey

Sometimes, God will take away some things, people, or valuables for you to realize what and who you needed all the while long.

-Kala Jordan-Lindsey

Valuables are not more powerful than the Lord.

-Kala Jordan-Lindsey

Sometimes, you have to lose something or someone for you to appreciate life more than you did the day before.

-Kala Jordan-Lindsey

The good fight is medicine to strengthen your spiritual walk in Jesus Christ.

-Kala Jordan-Lindsey

Not everyone will like you, but God will always love you.

-Kala Jordan-Lindsey

Sometimes, God will take everything you have so you can embrace everything He created you with.

-Kala Jordan-Lindsey

Feed your heart positive words and watch it bloom into what God intended.

-Kala Jordan-Lindsey

The person who perseveres will overcome life.

-Kala Jordan-Lindsey

Your deepest thoughts may be the book your hands are waiting to write.

-Kala Jordan-Lindsey

There's a greater reason in every tough season, beyond human understanding. Trust God's plan.

-Kala Jordan-Lindsey

The best way to cope with your temporary seasons is to be thankful and embrace each day like never before.

-Kala Jordan-Lindsey

Embrace the grace in your mistakes.

-Kala Jordan-Lindsey

You are made of everything you choose to intake.

-Kala Jordan-Lindsey

The Most Powerful Quotes to Enhance Your Life

Count on God to find you a seat if you don't slow it down in life.

-Kala Jordan-Lindsey

Never let anyone stop you from dreaming and believing that you won't make it. You'll make it.

-Kala Jordan-Lindsey

You were born to succeed, so believe it and you will achieve it.

-Kala Jordan-Lindsey

Submit to your calling, not someone else's.

-Kala Jordan-Lindsey

If you're confused about your gifts, consult with God and He'll reveal them to you.

-Kala Jordan-Lindsey

Sometimes, experiencing a turning point is necessary so you can get to where God needs you to be for His glory.

-Kala Jordan-Lindsey

The Most Powerful Quotes to Enhance Your Life

Your breakthrough is your turning point. Get ready for it.

-Kala Jordan-Lindsey

That job is for you, and I know it. Now believe it.

-Kala Jordan-Lindsey

Grace always finds a way out. And if there isn't one, God will make one.

-Kala Jordan-Lindsey

Run until you reach the finish line.

-Kala Jordan-Lindsey

Better days are here, and better days are approaching.

-Kala Jordan-Lindsey

God's abilities will always outweigh your disabilities.

-Kala Jordan-Lindsey

When you struggle with life, you become purposely stronger.

-Kala Jordan-Lindsey

Jesus will cover you when no one has your back.

-Kala Jordan-Lindsey

God can deposit what you'll never be able to do into your life.

-Kala Jordan-Lindsey

Focus on Jesus instead of the problem.

-Kala Jordan-Lindsey

If you're still breathing with open eyes and can hear your heart beating, you're blessed.

-Kala Jordan-Lindsey

Embrace your final days, months, and years before it's too late.

-Kala Jordan-Lindsey

The Most Powerful Quotes to Enhance Your Life

You've got so much to live for, so be brave.

-Kala Jordan-Lindsey

Reach for the stars and never stop rising.

-Kala Jordan-Lindsey

You can do it, but God will make it happen.

-Kala Jordan-Lindsey

Be bold before you grow old.

-Kala Jordan-Lindsey

You're young and beautiful, so stop complaining.

-Kala Jordan-Lindsey

Be thankful because God has already made a way.

-Kala Jordan-Lindsey

Desiring a closer relationship in Christ is far more profitable than gaining wealth without the Lord's guidance.

-Kala Jordan-Lindsey

There's always hope at the edge of the cliff, at the bottom of the mountain, and at the end of the tunnel.

-Kala Jordan-Lindsey

Worry, and you'll have a mental wreck.

-Kala Jordan-Lindsey

You have nothing to lose and everything to gain in Jesus Christ.

-Kala Jordan-Lindsey

Bless others and God will continue to bless you.

-Kala Jordan-Lindsey

The Most Powerful Quotes to Enhance Your Life

God allows unexpected storms to happen to strengthen your faith.

-Kala Jordan-Lindsey

Be determined to keep going no matter what.

-Kala Jordan-Lindsey

You're on the run because you're chasing everything except Jesus.

-Kala Jordan-Lindsey

It takes little to write a book, but faith to release your passion.

-Kala Jordan-Lindsey

Write with faith, not fear.

-Kala Jordan-Lindsey

Let your uncomfortable seasons of life strengthen your mental health one day at a time.

-Kala Jordan-Lindsey

A person with a humble heart is a great listener.

-Kala Jordan-Lindsey

If you start with prayer, your day will be better.

-Kala Jordan-Lindsey

Let God control your heartbeat. He's the only One that'll make sure it's in rhythm.

-Kala Jordan-Lindsey

If you live in rhythm with God, you'll hear His voice.

-Kala Jordan-Lindsey

Seek counseling because you're paranoid, causing you to lose your mind.

-Kala Jordan-Lindsey

Have a moment of silence each day. It'll build up your well-being.

-Kala Jordan-Lindsey

The passion to write and publish does not discriminate; it's a gift planted in every human being's heart that has the power to do the unimaginable.

-Kala Jordan-Lindsey

Settle your trust in the Lord's hands.

-Kala Jordan-Lindsey

I enjoy your company. Your spirit is unlike the world.

-Kala Jordan-Lindsey

You changed my mind, but God transformed my life.

-Kala Jordan-Lindsey

Change your attitude, or something severe will happen.

-Kala Jordan-Lindsey

If you don't get the job, promotion, business loan, or book deal, keep the faith without faltering.

-Kala Jordan-Lindsey

Stop thinking about tomorrow; embrace today—this precious moment.

-Kala Jordan-Lindsey

Date nights are a time to forget about the clock and enjoy life to the fullest.

-Kala Jordan-Lindsey

The more you save and invest, the earlier you can retire.

-Kala Jordan-Lindsey

Apples aren't the only thing teachers love. They also enjoy Cuban food.

-Kala Jordan-Lindsey

Be conscious of your mind, body, and soul.

-Kala Jordan-Lindsey

Focus on making an impact.

-Kala Jordan-Lindsey

You're one out of over a billion other human beings on the planet with something special to offer.

-Kala Jordan-Lindsey

You have the power and potential to change lives.

-Kala Jordan-Lindsey

Stand out because you brighten the day.

-Kala Jordan-Lindsey

Your stories matter, so release them.

-Kala Jordan-Lindsey

Grab a pencil and be quiet.

-Kala Jordan-Lindsey

You don't need permission to publish your story. Release it with faith.

-Kala Jordan-Lindsey

Your testimonies matter, so glorify God.

-Kala Jordan-Lindsey

Be empowered to achieve your goals without waiting for someone's permission.

-Kala Jordan-Lindsey

Your valuable life matters, so give it your all.

-Kala Jordan-Lindsey

Your voice is unique, so sing out loud.

-Kala Jordan-Lindsey

Writing is medicine for the mind, body, and soul. I'm convinced because I've tasted its reality.

-Kala Jordan-Lindsey

Writing is a world worth experiencing. Turn right and write.

-Kala Jordan-Lindsey

Writing a book is like giving birth; embrace your deliverance.

-Kala Jordan-Lindsey

Celebrate your life on purpose because you were created and blessed with purpose by Purpose, Jesus Christ.

-Kala Jordan-Lindsey

Don't apologize for your imperfections. God created you on purpose.

-Kala Jordan-Lindsey

Desire to celebrate life despite your circumstances.

-Kala Jordan-Lindsey

Take care of your body, or it'll be too late.

-Kala Jordan-Lindsey

A healthier lifestyle will improve other areas of your life.

-Kala Jordan-Lindsey

Life is a process; enjoy every moment and opportunity that comes your way before you close your eyes.

-Kala Jordan-Lindsey

You can't turn back the hands of time, but you can enjoy the moment you have right now.

-Kala Jordan-Lindsey

Live with an attitude of gratitude in accepting rejection. It's not a failure, a curse, or bad news when you know there's something better awaiting you—a greater reason.

-Kala Jordan-Lindsey

Expect God to say yes, but don't fret when He says no.

-Kala Jordan-Lindsey

God will carry you to your destination.

-Kala Jordan-Lindsey

There's power in your complicated life.

-Kala Jordan-Lindsey

You're young and blessed. Stop complaining.

-Kala Jordan-Lindsey

Embrace each chapter of your life.

-Kala Jordan-Lindsey

Hug, smile, and encourage every child you see and speak to daily. They're human, too.

-Kala Jordan-Lindsey

While you're writing your plans, remember God's plan will overrule your plans.

-Kala Jordan-Lindsey

Your kind attitude will carry you a long way in life.

-Kala Jordan-Lindsey

Never let negativity influence your choices and determine your tomorrow. You're stronger than words and fear.

-Kala Jordan-Lindsey

It's okay to make mistakes; you're human.

-Kala Jordan-Lindsey

New beginnings are the best.

-Kala Jordan-Lindsey

You will make it to the other side.

-Kala Jordan-Lindsey

Don't be silent; open your mouth.

-Kala Jordan-Lindsey

Your perseverance inspires others.

-Kala Jordan-Lindsey

God knows best, so hang in there and never give up.

-Kala Jordan-Lindsey

Speak confidently with your beautiful voice.

-Kala Jordan-Lindsey

Your greatest fear is stopping you from enjoying life.

-Kala Jordan-Lindsey

Be thankful because God blessed you with another day that you didn't deserve.

-Kala Jordan-Lindsey

Life may pull you down, but God will bless you to rise.

-Kala Jordan-Lindsey

You're going to make it, so stay on track.

-Kala Jordan-Lindsey

The Most Powerful Quotes to Enhance Your Life

Your human side is beautiful.

    -Kala Jordan-Lindsey

Expect a rainbow after the storm.

    -Kala Jordan-Lindsey

Celebrate every milestone because you deserve it.

    -Kala Jordan-Lindsey

You can do it, baby.

    -Kala Jordan-Lindsey

Stay strong, and trust in God's process.

-Kala Jordan-Lindsey

It's not over, even when it seems like it might be. God still has a purpose for your life.

-Kala Jordan-Lindsey

Pray silently and fight loudly.

-Kala Jordan-Lindsey

Passion doesn't depend on the world. It depends on you.

-Kala Jordan-Lindsey

Passion is a gift revealed and confirmed to you by God.

-Kala Jordan-Lindsey

Hug me tighter because I love you.

-Kala Jordan-Lindsey

Make love like never before because God has empowered you to in marriage.

-Kala Jordan-Lindsey

Passion is from within; it's hidden in the heart.

-Kala Jordan-Lindsey

Passion is activated when you let your heart and mind work together.

-Kala Jordan-Lindsey

Your passion is performed with an outburst.

-Kala Jordan-Lindsey

You were born to dream with purpose, power, and passion.

-Kala Jordan-Lindsey

When life gets tough, embrace it. You don't know what God is holding in store for you.

-Kala Jordan-Lindsey

Walk with an attitude of gratitude because you're not supposed to be here.

-Kala Jordan-Lindsey

If you ever feel like giving up or like there's nothing and no one worth living for, just sit down and listen to your heartbeat.

-Kala Jordan-Lindsey

Never forget to laugh out loud.

-Kala Jordan-Lindsey

From the moment you open your eyes until you close them. That's what makes you special.

-Kala Jordan-Lindsey

God is good, even when man looks down on us with nothing good or positive to say.

-Kala Jordan-Lindsey

God has His eyes on you, so stay focused on Him.

-Kala Jordan-Lindsey

God has the power to turn your life around.

-Kala Jordan-Lindsey

Your life reflects your actions.

-Kala Jordan-Lindsey

Your lifestyle is pleasing to the Lord.

-Kala Jordan-Lindsey

You build others up through your love.

-Kala Jordan-Lindsey

Your spirit makes the world a better place.

-Kala Jordan-Lindsey

Your attitude is contagious.

-Kala Jordan-Lindsey

Your hugs have the power to comfort others.

-Kala Jordan-Lindsey

There's always Light at the end of the tunnel. Look for Him.

-Kala Jordan-Lindsey

Keep living until your final breath.

-Kala Jordan-Lindsey

Strive to fulfill your purpose in life.

-Kala Jordan-Lindsey

Be thankful for every heartbeat, or you may miss one.

-Kala Jordan-Lindsey

Love more and you'll live longer.

-Kala Jordan-Lindsey

You're appreciated as big as the earth.

-Kala Jordan-Lindsey

Don't let anybody remove the good, hope, and faith from your heart.

-Kala Jordan-Lindsey

Prayer comforts the heart and spreads to thousands.

-Kala Jordan-Lindsey

Pray even when life seems dark; study the Light.

-Kala Jordan-Lindsey

Money can't buy love, but you can express your passion for life by investing in great books that'll add value to your walk.

-Kala Jordan-Lindsey

You're a special hero to the world.

-Kala Jordan-Lindsey

You're special like the sunshine after the storm.

-Kala Jordan-Lindsey

Friendships last forever if they're real.

-Kala Jordan-Lindsey

God gives breakthroughs, so expect yours to happen.

-Kala Jordan-Lindsey

The Most Powerful Quotes to Enhance Your Life

You make my day when you smile.

-Kala Jordan-Lindsey

You inspire the poor because you understand the significance of God's word.

-Kala Jordan-Lindsey

Pray for the loud voices screaming for help on this planet.

-Kala Jordan-Lindsey

The Most Powerful Quotes to Enhance Your Life

Be hopeful because great things will happen to you this year.

-Kala Jordan-Lindsey

Let silence inspire you to be thankful with what you already have and what is yet to come.

-Kala Jordan-Lindsey

God's love satisfies my appetite.

-Kala Jordan-Lindsey

You're blessed to see the sun, so give it your all.

-Kala Jordan-Lindsey

Forgive me. It was a mistake.

-Kala Jordan-Lindsey

Walk purposely while making the best of every opportunity and blessing given to you from God.

-Kala Jordan-Lindsey

There's nothing more powerful than embracing God's grace and mercy in storms.

-Kala Jordan-Lindsey

Release the tension in your heart because it's affecting your happiness.

-Kala Jordan-Lindsey

Don't stress about tomorrow; live for today.

-Kala Jordan-Lindsey

The Most Powerful Quotes to Enhance Your Life

Embrace your turning point when you reach it.

-Kala Jordan-Lindsey

You can't turn your life around. God can.

-Kala Jordan-Lindsey

Your pain has blessed you with power to help encourage others.

-Kala Jordan-Lindsey

The Most Powerful Quotes to Enhance Your Life

Having peace in the world will never bring you authentic joy and satisfaction because real peace is found in Jesus Christ.

-Kala Jordan-Lindsey

Let your insecurities remind you how beautiful you are to God.

-Kala Jordan-Lindsey

You're a winner in Christ, so don't be discouraged when you lose on earth.

-Kala Jordan-Lindsey

The Most Powerful Quotes to Enhance Your Life

One of the greatest things you can ever do in life is to never give up.

-Kala Jordan-Lindsey

Your passion is a treasure that's revealed to you by God.

-Kala Jordan-Lindsey

God blessed you with a calling to help others who need encouragement in their calling.

-Kala Jordan-Lindsey

There's purpose in your hardships, so endure God's will.

-Kala Jordan-Lindsey

Love God, first, then yourself and others.

-Kala Jordan-Lindsey

Don't bury your calling; share it with the world before it's too late.

-Kala Jordan-Lindsey

The Most Powerful Quotes to Enhance Your Life

In pain, God will strengthen your purpose. So, embrace the thorns.

-Kala Jordan-Lindsey

Turn your feelings into books to uplift others in their difficult seasons of life.

-Kala Jordan-Lindsey

Write someone a thank you note and smile.

-Kala Jordan-Lindsey

Your determination is impressive, like your performance.

-Kala Jordan-Lindsey

There are amazing blessings and purpose in every rejection.

-Kala Jordan-Lindsey

Your failures will hinder your progress if you don't move forward.

-Kala Jordan-Lindsey

I love your style. It's mind-blowing.

-Kala Jordan-Lindsey

A person who's ungrateful for life has a difficult time resting.

-Kala Jordan-Lindsey

Be thankful a thousand times more than you were yesterday.

-Kala Jordan-Lindsey

Speak out; share your voice and express yourself.

-Kala Jordan-Lindsey

God blessed you with a powerful mind to lead others in the right direction.

-Kala Jordan-Linsey

If you ever feel that you can't go on, restart again.

-Kala Jordan-Lindsey

The Most Powerful Quotes to Enhance Your Life

God will show up and show out for you.

-Kala Jordan-Lindsey

Let God quiet your heart.

-Kala Jordan-Lindsey

God will help you complete the task if you let Him.

-Kala Jordan-Lindsey

You can do it if you never give up on this journey.

-Kala Jordan-Lindsey

You will make it. Believe and expect.

-Kala Jordan-Lindsey

Spice up your sex life by being creative, and you'll enjoy it every time.

-Kala Jordan-Lindsey

Love longer than your age.

-Kala Jordan-Lindsey

Love deeper than the ocean.

-Kala Jordan-Lindsey

God's love spreads like a virus.

-Kala Jordan-Lindsey

Write a love story and share it with others. The world can never receive too much love.

-Kala Jordan-Lindsey

Be inspired by someone else's story.

-Kala Jordan-Lindsey

You inspire millions like the rainbow in the sky.

-Kala Jordan-Lindsey

Your worth weighs more than the universe.

-Kala Jordan-Lindsey

Make the best each day as if it were your last.

-Kala Jordan-Lindsey

You're stronger than every muscle in your body.

-Kala Jordan-Lindsey

Your good-hearted spirit is as contagious as a cold.

-Kala Jordan-Lindsey

Your passion for life draws others close to you.

-Kala Jordan-Lindsey

It's more powerful to fight with the Word of God than with powerless weapons.

-Kala Jordan-Lindsey

You're standing because God is not ready for you to rest.

-Kala Jordan-Lindsey

You're a survivor who holds more power than you think, so go out into the world and encourage someone with hope.

-Kala Jordan-Lindsey

Exercise every book out of your soul and through your fingers by simply writing because you're on fire to share your deep stories like your most desirable cravings.

-Kala Jordan-Lindsey

If you're ever in the ring of life and feel like quitting, just know you will always win the battle with a strong mindset.

-Kala Jordan-Lindsey

God's life support is more precious and powerful than your problems.

-Kala Jordan-Lindsey

The Most Powerful Quotes to Enhance Your Life

You have the power to overcome depression if you believe it and rise.

-Kala Jordan-Lindsey

You're extraordinary and unique because God chose you to walk.

-Kala Jordan-Lindsey

You were chosen not because the color of your skin, but because of God's grace and mercy over your life.

-Kala Jordan-Lindsey

You're never alone because the Creator of the world lives within you if you believe it.

-Kala Jordan-Lindsey

Rise and do something productive with your life because many are dying to be inspired by your story.

-Kala Jordan-Lindsey

Just because you don't have what you want, doesn't mean you'll never be blessed with what God planned for you to have.

-Kala Jordan-Lindsey

Once you discover our Heavenly Father, your life will no longer be the same.

-Kala Jordan-Lindsey

Keep your eyes open or else you'll be blind.

-Kala Jordan-Lindsey

The Most Powerful Quotes to Enhance Your Life

Find joy in your mistakes.

-Kala Jordan-Lindsey

Man can change, but God has sovereign power to transform lives.

-Kala Jordan-Lindsey

You don't need a makeover. If you're serious about your spiritual relationship in Christ, He'll transform you, one day at a time.

-Kala Jordan-Lindsey

The Most Powerful Quotes to Enhance Your Life

The best position on the planet is in Jesus Christ, so rejoice.

-Kala Jordan-Lindsey

Hook up with Jesus. He'll never break up with you.

-Kala Jordan-Lindsey

Be fired up in the Lord.

-Kala Jordan-Lindsey

If you're lonely, call on Jesus. He'll answer.

—Kala Jordan-Lindsey

Your heart stands out like the glitter on my fingers.

—Kala Jordan-Lindsey

If you're humble, God will open doors for you where doors were shut for others.

—Kala Jordan-Lindsey

The Most Powerful Quotes to Enhance Your Life

Listen before you face trouble.

-Kala Jordan-Lindsey

God will protect you. He's more significant than your enemies.

-Kala Jordan-Lindsey

You make me feel better; you're more powerful than a psychologist.

-Kala Jordan-Lindsey

You rock the world when you speak, so speak up and speak out.

-Kala Jordan-Lindsey

The choices you make today will have an impact on your tomorrow.

-Kala Jordan-Lindsey

Sweat with joy; it's healthy for you.

-Kala Jordan-Lindsey

The Most Powerful Quotes to Enhance Your Life

Spiritual food is more powerful than riches and fame.

-Kala Jordan-Lindsey

The Lord is calling you to turn your life over to Him, so don't send Him to voicemail. Answer the call.

-Kala Jordan-Lindsey

Stay in the Lord and never go astray.

-Kala Jordan-Lindsey

Nourishing your spiritual health will help strengthen your mental health—that's a fact.

-Kala Jordan-Lindsey

Slow it down and embrace the simple life.

-Kala Jordan-Lindsey

Writing has the power to quench your heart. So, release that stuff out of your system.

-Kala Jordan-Lindsey

Let positivity motivate you to be better than yesterday.

-Kala Jordan-Lindsey

Just because no one is cheering for you doesn't mean you're not liked. God loves you, which is all that matters.

-Kala Jordan-Lindsey

There's someone Greater in the audience, so stay focused.

-Kala Jordan-Lindsey

The Most Powerful Quotes to Enhance Your Life

God is cheering for you.

-Kala Jordan-Lindsey

You're sweet, like my favorite fruits.

-Kala Jordan-Lindsey

Life is too precious to quit now.

-Kala Jordan-Lindsey

The Most Powerful Quotes to Enhance Your Life

When you worship and glorify God, He'll bless you mentally, physically, and spiritually. He'll bless your life.

-Kala Jordan-Lindsey

Every time God blesses you is an experience worth praising Him for.

-Kala Jordan-Lindsey

Living in Christ will have you hooked for life.

-Kala-Jordan-Lindsey

Life is a problem, but if you want to experience true life, you must follow the real formula.

-Kala Jordan-Lindsey

Sometimes, it's not the first sentence that makes it happen, but the last, because it proves results.

-Kala Jordan-Lindsey

To comfort others is not only a blessing, but it's a special, purposeful, and powerful gift we can give others in times of need.

-Kala Jordan-Lindsey

Embrace today as if it were your last.

-Kala Jordan-Lindsey

Pray through your failures and success.

-Kala Jordan-Lindsey

The Most Powerful Quotes to Enhance Your Life

Your life calling will always reveal itself to be more fulfilling and powerful than your wildest dreams.

-Kala Jordan-Lindsey

Life is not as hard as you think if you take it one day at a time. Stay strong in the Lord.

-Kala Jordan-Lindsey

Think bigger and it'll happen.

-Kala Jordan-Lindsey

Living with a humble heart in the sight of the Lord has the power to transform all areas of your life and lifestyle in many ways than you ever imagined.

-Kala Jordan-Lindsey

God will make a way out of no way. So, trust Him over your issues.

-Kala Jordan-Lindsey

God gives the best benefits.

-Kala Jordan-Lindsey

You're brave, so go for it and have faith.

-Kala Jordan-Lindsey

Living in Christ is more powerful than just inhaling and exhaling.

-Kala Jordan-Lindsey

Don't hide your pain. Share your story with others.

-Kala Jordan-Lindsey

God orchestrates life events to shift you where you need to be for His glory.

-Kala Jordan-Lindsey

Use your voice to help be the change in the world.

-Kala Jordan-Lindsey

You matter, so get up and act like it.

-Kala Jordan-Lindsey

Chase the Source, not the resources and you'll be more appreciative of life.

-Kala Jordan-Lindsey

I see your efforts. You're doing a wonderful job.

-Kala Jordan-Lindsey

The Most Powerful Quotes to Enhance Your Life

We never realize how blessed we are, and we don't recognize the sparkling jewel that God created in us until we've experienced enough storms.

-Kala Jordan-Lindsey

Cherish your mind, or it'll fail you.

-Kala Jordan-Lindsey

You blossom every time I see you.

-Kala Jordan-Lindsey

Your breakthrough is on the way. So, don't be discouraged and doubt God's mighty power. Instead, be confident, and expect His grace.

-Kala Jordan-Lindsey

Take good care of your body and embrace every moment you're temporarily in it.

-Kala Jordan-Lindsey

The Most Powerful Quotes to Enhance Your Life

It's never too late to learn and improve in all areas of your life. Go for it.

-Kala Jordan-Lindsey

Not everything we see, and desire is good for our mind, body, and soul.

-Kala Jordan-Lindsey

To write a good book is simple, but to write a powerful book takes heart and more than you'd ever imagine. You can do it.

-Kala Jordan-Lindsey

Let God control the steering wheel of your life. He doesn't need you.

-Kala Jordan-Lindsey

God has the power to bless you without your strength.

-Kala Jordan-Lindsey

Don't feed your mind, body, and soul junk. Always protect your temple.

-Kala Jordan-Lindsey

Writing is like love making; it permits you to be free and control the pen.

-Kala Jordan-Lindsey

Writing allows you to express your deepest thoughts and feelings.

-Kala Jordan-Lindsey

The Most Powerful Quotes to Enhance Your Life

You're not alone. God is closer to you than the sun.

-Kala Jordan-Lindsey

Negative influences will destroy your life, so be careful what you feed your heart.

-Kala Jordan-Lindsey

Sometimes, the smallest things can have the greatest impact in your life.

-Kala Jordan-Lindsey

Kick your feet up and relax your mind.

-Kala Jordan-Lindsey

Your authenticity engages me.

-Kala Jordan-Lindsey

Take your time and never give up. You'll make it.

-Kala Jordan-Lindsey

You've come too far to quit, so keep going.

-Kala Jordan-Lindsey

There's only one of you, so give it all you have before it's over.

-Kala Jordan-Lindsey

Only God can heal a broken heart—one day at a time with faith.

-Kala Jordan-Lindsey

The Most Powerful Quotes to Enhance Your Life

Love yourself to the end.

-Kala Jordan-Lindsey

Don't let anyone disturb your peace in the Lord.

-Kala Jordan-Lindsey

Submit to your calling, or you'll struggle to make a living.

-Kala Jordan-Lindsey

Stand up, and God will carry you through your storms with His mighty power.

-Kala Jordan-Lindsey

The blessing of true life is an extraordinary gift.

-Kala Jordan-Lindsey

The Most Powerful Quotes to Enhance Your Life

God never misses His sleigh rides; He's always on time, knows what's best for our lives, and blesses us with our every need.

-Kala Jordan-Lindsey

A divorce may cause you emotional distress unless you're prepared to accept God's will.

-Kala Jordan-Lindsey

Train your thoughts to be positive. Then, maybe you'll be happier.

-Kala Jordan-Lindsey

Write a book because you deserve to leave your story behind.

-Kala Jordan-Lindsey

Don't be discouraged. There's hope for what you don't have.

-Kala Jordan-Lindsey

The very no is always the perfect and powerful yes.

-Kala Jordan-Lindsey

You're beautiful like a garden.

-Kala Jordan-Lindsey

When unexpectedness knocks on your door, be prepared to be still and trust the Lord.

-Kala Jordan-Lindsey

The Most Powerful Quotes to Enhance Your Life

There's a reason why your heart is still beating. Never take it for granted. Embrace it and give it wisely, before it's too late.

-Kala Jordan-Lindsey

We all have goals, but not everyone is willing to do what it takes to achieve them. If you're on a mission to complete a task or accomplish a goal, eliminate distractions and stay focused. Have faith that you will succeed.

-Kala Jordan-Lindsey

If you're going through a storm, see the blessing and, more important, purpose in your difficulties; let God guide you where you need to be because He will. And think positive. It'll strengthen your mind.

-Kala Jordan-Lindsey

Your heart will always be louder than your voice.

-Kala Jordan-Lindsey

God will strengthen your marriage if you trust His power.

-Kala Jordan-Lindsey

Let your weaknesses empower you to overcome your next battle in life.

-Kala Jordan-Lindsey

Be wise before you face a dead end.

-Kala Jordan-Lindsey

You received more grace than you've struggled. Be thankful because it could have been worst.

-Kala Jordan-Lindsey

Positive advice comforts a broken heart.

-Kala Jordan-Lindsey

Leave the world behind and follow Jesus.

-Kala Jordan-Lindsey

The Most Powerful Quotes to Enhance Your Life

Be careful not to judge a person with mental health issues because we're all imperfect.

-Kala Jordan-Lindsey

Writing gives you the freedom and fun to express, convince, and give yourself to others without limitations.

-Kala Jordan-Lindsey

If you're going through a storm, see the blessing and, more important, purpose in your difficulties; let God guide you where you need to be because He will. And think positive. It'll strengthen your mind.

-Kala Jordan-Lindsey

Take a step back and pray about your intentions for starting a business.

-Kala Jordan-Lindsey

Each day, strive to be better than you were yesterday.

-Kala Jordan-Lindsey

Follow the Leader, not the crowd.

-Kala Jordan-Lindsey

Early mornings and late nights are the most amazing and effective times to write.

-Kala Jordan-Lindsey

Take a day off because you deserve it.

-Kala Jordan-Lindsey

You're worth more than your valuables.

-Kala Jordan-Lindsey

Don't bury your life; share it before your final breath.

-Kala Jordan-Lindsey

Your personality blesses the ungodly.

-Kala Jordan-Lindsey

A real friend will go the extra mile to support you.

-Kala Jordan-Lindsey

Storms will strengthen your weaknesses.

-Kala Jordan-Lindsey

The Most Powerful Quotes to Enhance Your Life

You're not fighting alone. God is in the ring with you. So, stand up and walk.

-Kala Jordan-Lindsey

We must make the rest of our lives the best of our lives with unwavering hope and faith in the Lord.

-Kala Jordan-Lindsey

Your cheerful spirit calms my heart.

-Kala Jordan-Lindsey

Never giving up is part of the process of overcoming obstacles.

-Kala Jordan-Lindsey

True success starts and finishes with God.

-Kala Jordan-Lindsey

Real success starts with faith.

-Kala Jordan-Lindsey

The Most Powerful Quotes to Enhance Your Life

To never give up takes a strong, focused, and healthy heart and mindset.

-Kala Jordan-Lindsey

God will elevate you when you sit down.

-Kala Jordan-Lindsey

Overcoming fear is a great accomplishment.

-Kala Jordan-Lindsey

The Most Powerful Quotes to Enhance Your Life

You don't have to believe in everyone's religion or spiritual beliefs, but you can still learn to love, respect, and appreciate your neighbors.

-Kala Jordan-Lindsey

Don't live and desire to compete with others for recognition.

-Kala Jordan-Lindsey

Climb until you triumph.

-Kala Jordan-Lindsey

The Most Powerful Quotes to Enhance Your Life

Be beautiful because you are.

-Kala Jordan-Lindsey

There is comfort in silence, but peace and blessings when you shine your light and sing your songs.

-Kala Jordan-Lindsey

Life will never be the same without you.

-Kala Jordan-Lindsey

Mistakes are okay unless you continue making the same ones intentionally.

-Kala Jordan-Lindsey

Though life would be better if we all owned a million dollars, it would be different and unusual because there wouldn't be competitions, struggles, obstacles, or anything to strive for. There wouldn't be a reason to give God all the praise, glory, and honor that He's worthy of receiving.

-Kala Jordan-Lindsey

The Most Powerful Quotes to Enhance Your Life

Guide the poor to God, who nourishes our souls.

-Kala Jordan-Lindsey

Sometimes you must learn to let go and move on.

-Kala Jordan-Lindsey

Following the world leads to depression and destruction.

-Kala Jordan-Lindsey

The Most Powerful Quotes to Enhance Your Life

Sometimes, the biggest storms you experience produce the greatest and most powerful blessings.

-Kala Jordan-Lindsey

Jesus is the answer and He's the only One who can fix whatever problem you're facing.

-Kala Jordan-Lindsey

Seek Him, His will, and He'll help you solve your problems.

-Kala Jordan-Lindsey

Sometimes, God will stop your plans to reveal His plans so that He can open doors in your life.

-Kala Jordan-Lindsey

When it seems dark, remember the true Light.

-Kala Jordan-Lindsey

You're doing too much. Slow it down, or life will.

-Kala Jordan-Lindsey

The moment you embrace the Light in darkness is the moment God will begin to open your eyes; you'll gain spiritual vision.

-Kala Jordan-Lindsey

Difficult roads lead to beautiful destinations. So, wherever you are in the storm, keep going and never give up.

-Kala Jordan-Lindsey

Desire to live with open eyes.

-Kala Jordan-Lindsey

The Most Powerful Quotes to Enhance Your Life

Anxiety is just a false alarm to the fears of life. So, be aware and you'll overcome this monster.

-Kala Jordan-Lindsey

Compliment your neighbors with positive words.

-Kala Jordan-Lindsey

There's always a rainbow after every storm. You have to search for it.

-Kala Jordan-Lindsey

Christ is the greatest, most powerful prescription on the market, in the world, and on the planet.

-Kala Jordan-Lindsey

During your waiting period, God is preparing you for what's going to blow your mind, so never give up while you're waiting for Him to move.

-Kala Jordan-Lindsey

Turn to Jesus, and He'll change your name.

-Kala Jordan-Lindsey

You were created on purpose, with purpose, and for a greater purpose to rise, not to run.

-Kala Jordan-Lindsey

Sometimes, God will take you through a storm to prepare you for a mind-blowing, spiritual blessing.

-Kala Jordan-Lindsey

The Most Powerful Quotes to Enhance Your Life

Thrive without having self-doubt.

-Kala Jordan-Lindsey

Your walk today will have an impact on your life and the lives of others for years to come.

-Kala Jordan-Lindsey

Don't ever let your neighborhood define where you're headed in life.

-Kala Jordan-Lindsey

God is bigger than your location; He's greater than your address, and more powerful than your environment.

-Kala Jordan-Lindsey

You exist because you were created to do great things in life before you no longer exist.

-Kala Jordan-Lindsey

You thought losing your job was the worst thing ever, but God saw it as one of the best things that could have happened.

-Kala Jordan-Lindsey

You see the worst in you, but God sees the best in you.

-Kala Jordan-Lindsey

God has the power to turn your battle into a blessing.

-Kala Jordan-Lindsey

The Most Powerful Quotes to Enhance Your Life

Find joy in the uncomfortable aspects of life.

-Kala Jordan-Lindsey

Be creative like mixing blue and yellow of the rainbow.

-Kala Jordan-Lindsey

With God, all things are possible, so never give up no matter how stressful or chaotic life gets, and no matter how dark the road looks.

-Kala Jordan-Lindsey

When you're in a tight situation and you don't know what to do or how you're going to make it through the hour, expect God's grace and mercy to bless you in your darkest moments of life.

-Kala Jordan-Lindsey

Don't panic in the middle of the test. It's just a "test" to check your faith. Stay focused. You'll make it to the end.

-Kala Jordan-Lindsey

The Most Powerful Quotes to Enhance Your Life

The moment you find joy in your storms is the moment you become fulfilled; your soul is quenched because you've learned how to embrace the lemons in life.

-Kala Jordan-Lindsey

Never doubt because God created you with power to have faith in any situation.

-Kala Jordan-Lindsey

The Most Powerful Quotes to Enhance Your Life

Anyone can write, but not everyone can "make love" on the page.

-Kala Jordan-Lindsey

Sometimes an unfortunate "no" is the greatest blessing that could ever happened.

-Kala Jordan-Lindsey

Spankings are blessings from the Lord; they aren't intended to hurt you except help you. So, embrace the experience.

-Kala Jordan-Lindsey

Brown is beautiful like the rainbow that shines after the storm.

-Kala Jordan-Lindsey

The good thing about mistakes is that Grace gives you another chance—another opportunity.

-Kala Jordan-Lindsey

Love others beyond as many times God has blessed you.

-Kala Jordan-Lindsey

The mind is a precious gift to abandon. Nourish it with the word of God.

-Kala Jordan-Lindsey

The Most Powerful Quotes to Enhance Your Life

Rock bottom experiences should make you stronger and wiser like accidents.

-Kala Jordan-Lindsey

Listening to music relaxes your mind and uplifts an agitated spirit.

-Kala Jordan-Lindsey

Life is like a puzzle; each piece goes exactly where it should be along the journey.

-Kala Jordan-Lindsey

The Most Powerful Quotes to Enhance Your Life

You must struggle before you win.

-Kala Jordan-Lindsey

Three positive words have the power to encourage someone over four hundred pages of myths.

-Kala Jordan-Lindsey

Your scariest turn may be the greatest turn you ever make.

-Kala Jordan-Lindsey

Positive words comfort the heart, but harsh words depress the mind.

-Kala Jordan-Lindsey

When God is ready to bless you, He knows who and what to send.

-Kala Jordan-Lindsey

Embrace the discomfort; life is not meant to be comfortable.

-Kala Jordan-Lindsey

The Most Powerful Quotes to Enhance Your Life

Your breakthrough is right in front of you. Embrace it.

-Kala Jordan-Lindsey

You don't need a million words to get your point across. Just write and publish. Your neighbor is waiting to read your story.

-Kala Jordan-Lindsey

When you're in tune, clicked, connected, and in sync with Jesus, everything else falls into place.

-Kala Jordan-Lindsey

Think of ways to do positive things for others.

-Kala Jordan-Lindsey

If you know where you're going, look forward and stay focused.

-Kala Jordan-Lindsey

It takes effort to write, but it requires faith to write and publish a book.

-Kala Jordan-Lindsey

God can rescue you from anywhere in your life. Believe He can.

-Kala Jordan-Lindsey

It's dark inside and out, so keep shining your light when you rise.

-Kala Jordan-Lindsey

If at first you don't succeed, it's okay. Rise and try again.

-Kala Jordan-Lindsey

Embrace your mistakes, blemishes, and flaws. We're all imperfect, except our Heavenly Father.

-Kala Jordan-Lindsey

You have to fail before you can win.

-Kala Jordan-Lindsey

Your stamina motivates others with the hope of overcoming life.

-Kala Jordan-Lindsey

It takes a lifetime to heal, for some. So, don't expect to heal as fast as your neighbor.

-Kala Jordan-Lindsey

Embrace how God turns your struggles into passion.

-Kala Jordan-Lindsey

The Most Powerful Quotes to Enhance Your Life

Write after having sex. You'll be energized.

-Kala Jordan-Lindsey

Just because you've experienced a storm doesn't mean it's over.

-Kala Jordan-Lindsey

Fight through the storm and never give up.

-Kala Jordan-Lindsey

Your heart is healthier in Christ.

-Kala Jordan-Lindsey

Be positive. Stay positive. Embrace positivity.

-Kala Jordan-Lindsey

Be filled with energy because you never know when you'll need it.

-Kala Jordan-Lindsey

The Most Powerful Quotes to Enhance Your Life

Embrace the blessing of your storms.

-Kala Jordan-Lindsey

Unless you open your mouth, you can't be heard.

-Kala Jordan-Lindsey

Subscribe to prayer—it's more powerful than the person you're following.

-Kala Jordan-Lindsey

Determination will sustain you, but faith will get you there; it'll happen.

-Kala Jordan-Lindsey

Your love hour experience should be memorable.

-Kala Jordan-Lindsey

Like, love, and follow Jesus.

-Kala Jordan-Lindsey

The Most Powerful Quotes to Enhance Your Life

You have every reason to live because God has a purpose for your life.

-Kala Jordan-Lindsey

Your relationship in Christ has everything to do with your mental, physical, and spiritual health.

-Kala Jordan-Lindsey

The choices you make today will impact you every second of your life.

-Kala Jordan-Lindsey

Writing a book is a part of the healing process.

-Kala Jordan-Lindsey

There's something about a woman's hands that a man can never compare.

-Kala Jordan-Lindsey

Be encouraged when you struggle because God is in the midst of it all.

-Kala Jordan-Lindsey

Creative writing is like making love; it gives you freedom to express yourself.

-Kala Jordan-Lindsey

It doesn't matter where you've been and what you've faced, God can still do the impossible.

-Kala Jordan-Lindsey

A colorful wardrobe promotes positive thoughts.

-Kala Jordan-Lindsey

Wait for God to reveal His purpose in your pain because He will.

-Kala Jordan-Lindsey

The Most Powerful Quotes to Enhance Your Life

Sometimes the hardest part about writing a book is the deliverance. But like delivering a child, once you deliver, it's one of the greatest releases ever, like having the most powerful orgasm.

-Kala Jordan-Lindsey

Each day you're living, be thankful.

-Kala Jordan-Lindsey

The Most Powerful Quotes to Enhance Your Life

Live before it's too late to share what God destined for you to give to the world.

-Kala Jordan-Lindsey

Make yourself at home when you write.

-Kala Jordan-Lindsey

Forcing your way through life is like forcing a poem to rhyme. Don't force it; let it happen.

-Kala Jordan-Lindsey

A relationship is healthier in a positive environment.

-Kala Jordan-Lindsey

Don't panic, pray before you call the world.

-Kala Jordan-Lindsey

For every reason you complain, remember that someone else is doing worse.

-Kala Jordan-Lindsey

You're not crazy; you've lost your mind because you're not at peace in Christ.

-Kala Jordan-Lindsey

Clutter causes distractions and anxiety in your life if you're not conscious of your surroundings.

-Kala Jordan-Lindsey

You're mentally stronger when you're organized.

-Kala Jordan-Lindsey

The Most Powerful Quotes to Enhance Your Life

No matter how much we try, we'll never be able to get ourselves together because only God can.

    -Kala Jordan-Lindsey

Be cautious not to stray from God on this dark planet.

    -Kala Jordan-Lindsey

Eat healthier, then you'll feel better.

    -Kala Jordan-Lindsey

The Most Powerful Quotes to Enhance Your Life

A load of unnecessary stress causes health issues, so leave it at the door.

-Kala Jordan-Lindsey

Love is special; it's deeper than intimacy.

-Kala Jordan-Lindsey

Having a positive conversation with others strengthens your confidence and self-esteem.

-Kala Jordan-Lindsey

Focus more on how blessed you are rather than what you don't have. You'll start to appreciate life more than you ever imagined.

-Kala Jordan-Lindsey

Surround yourself with positive-minded friends that uplift you and encourage you in the good and in the bad.

-Kala Jordan-Lindsey

Uncomfortable experiences make you stronger and wiser.

-Kala Jordan-Lindsey

You're capable of doing more than you think you can.

-Kala Jordan-Lindsey

Desire peace over chaos.

-Kala Jordan-Lindsey

God is doing something great in your life, so look forward to what He has for you.

-Kala Jordan-Lindsey

Use your failures to bless others who are struggling with life.

-Kala Jordan-Lindsey

God will never take you anywhere He's never experienced, so be thankful wherever He takes you.

-Kala Jordan-Lindsey

You are beautiful inside and out—on your worst and bad days, and with or without makeup.

-Kala Jordan-Lindsey

God has something better for you so don't fret the small things that are out of your hand. Be thankful for what it is and move on with your life.

-Kala Jordan-Lindsey

The Most Powerful Quotes to Enhance Your Life

Exercise your faith so that others will be encouraged to turn their lives over to the Creator.

-Kala Jordan-Lindsey

When you rise you have a chance to help make a difference in the world.

-Kala Jordan-Lindsey

Setting goals boosts your confidence, and gives you hope for the future.

-Kala Jordan-Lindsey

Working hard forces you to do what may not be comfortable. But when you work smart, you'll be successful in life.

-Kala Jordan-Lindsey

Struggling with life is normal and blesses others.

-Kala Jordan-Lindsey

Work smart, and you'll succeed.

-Kala Jordan-Lindsey

Promote positivity, not drama in your life or others.

-Kala Jordan-Lindsey

You can never run away from storms in life, but you can prepare for the next one.

-Kala Jordan-Lindsey

Positive thinking produces healing and improves your overall health. So, invite only positive vibes into your life.

-Kala Jordan-Lindsey

Sometimes the greatest thing you love may be the most difficult blessing to let go.

-Kala Jordan-Lindsey

Promote peace or you'll have a hard time resting.

-Kala Jordan-Lindsey

An intimate relationship without God is unhealthy.

-Kala Jordan-Lindsey

Life has changed, things have changed, and people have changed. But God hasn't and never will.

-Kala Jordan-Lindsey

You don't need permission to publish your story; you're the story, so publish with faith.

-Kala Jordan-Lindsey

The Most Powerful Quotes to Enhance Your Life

Be thankful for the calling God has blessed you with....you're one of a kind.

-Kala Jordan-Lindsey

You don't need the perfect story; just write from the heart.

-Kala Jordan-Lindsey

You're more valuable than you think you are.

-Kala Jordan-Lindsey

Only God can do the impossible, so stay hopeful.

-Kala Jordan-Lindsey

If you want to sharpen your craft, work on it every day and help someone along the way.

-Kala Jordan-Lindsey

It's better to struggle in Christ than to fight without the Lord.

-Kala Jordan-Lindsey

If you're searching for a better way in life, keep going until you find Jesus.

-Kala Jordan-Lindsey

If you're unemployed, make use of your spiritual gifts for others and God will bless you in your calling.

-Kala Jordan-Lindsey

The Most Powerful Quotes to Enhance Your Life

Just a smile has the power to brighten someone's day, so keep smiling because yours is contagious.

-Kala Jordan-Lindsey

Writing a book takes more than you'll ever know unless you release your own.

-Kala Jordan-Lindsey

Let God change your weak mentality. He'll bless you if you allow Him to.

-Kala Jordan-Lindsey

Having sex in marriage helps you burn calories without going to the gym. So, if you're on a budget, have more sex at home.

-Kala Jordan-Lindsey

Living in the fast lane is risky and unhealthy, so slow it down or you'll crash.

-Kala Jordan-Lindsey

Don't criticize yourself; embrace your imperfections.

-Kala Jordan-Lindsey

Be original; be creative and express yourself.

-Kala Jordan-Lindsey

A mistake doesn't define your future. God already knows where He's taking you.

-Kala Jordan-Lindsey

Magnify God because you're one step closer to your dreams today than you were seven years ago.

-Kala Jordan-Lindsey

If your palms are sweaty and you have a lot on your mind, take some deep breaths and pray.

-Kala Jordan-Lindsey

In your dark seasons of life, embrace what you don't understand and seek God for guidance.

-Kala Jordan-Lindsey

Adopt a routine that improves your overall health.

-Kala Jordan-Lindsey

Leaving Jesus out of your schedule is like being alive without purpose.

-Kala Jordan-Lindsey

Teach because you inspire differently.

-Kala Jordan-Lindsey

Throw away the cigarettes and turn your life over to Jesus. He'll help you, not harm you.

-Kala Jordan-Lindsey

Celebrate your failures and accomplishments because your precious life matters more than you think.

-Kala Jordan-Lindsey

Wear your beauty marks with confidence because you can. You're beautiful inside and out.

-Kala Jordan-Lindsey

A dead end is just a resting spot; it's not the end because there's hope at difficult roads in life. Turn right and keep going with faith.

-Kala Jordan-Lindsey

The Most Powerful Quotes to Enhance Your Life

Rest, or you'll drain your precious health.

-Kala Jordan-Lindsey

Think positive, and you'll experience a better day.

-Kala Jordan-Lindsey

Your mind is like your heart; it's always with you, so nourish it with care and love.

-Kala Jordan-Lindsey

Don't complain and have a fit; keep walking until you arrive at your destination in life.

-Kala Jordan-Lindsey

Desire to do better and be better than you were yesterday because today might be your last.

-Kala Jordan-Lindsey

Develop a healthier routine, and you'll be satisfied.

-Kala Jordan-Lindsey

You're healthier when you're in your right mind.

-Kala Jordan-Lindsey

Don't eat a ton of burgers because you're unhappy with your life. Change your attitude; think positive and do something about it. Be motivated to improve your overall health for the better.

-Kala Jordan-Lindsey

The Most Powerful Quotes to Enhance Your Life

There are truly amazing people in the world. You're one of them.

-Kala Jordan-Lindsey

I adore your sassy spirit. You're filled with so much life and kindness that I'm inspired to make a change.

-Kala Jordan-Lindsey

The Most Powerful Quotes to Enhance Your Life

God always finds a way to get you one step closer to your destination if you trust in the process.

-Kala Jordan-Lindsey

Be a blessing to the world because change starts with you.

-Kala Jordan-Lindsey

The Most Powerful Quotes to Enhance Your Life

Boost your self-esteem and confidence by appreciating what it is—your strengths and weaknesses in life.

-Kala Jordan-Lindsey

Be authentic because there is no one like you and there never will be.

-Kala Jordan-Lindsey

A prideful heart shortens your life, so humble yourself.

-Kala Jordan-Lindsey

If at first you don't succeed, rise, and start with baby steps.

-Kala Jordan-Lindsey

Replace love with love, and love with more love.

-Kala Jordan-Lindsey

Let the world see the God in you instead of the person in the mirror—Monday through Sunday.

-Kala Jordan-Lindsey

This moment is significant, so cherish it.

-Kala Jordan-Lindsey

Drama causes frustration and anger. Welcome positive vibes into your life.

-Kala Jordan-Lindsey

Write someone a love letter…it just may help save a life.

-Kala Jordan-Lindsey

The easy part about exercising is starting, but being consistent is challenging. Exercise consistently for successful results.

-Kala Jordan-Lindsey

Your life is special, so, celebrate it. You weren't created to sit down and let your precious life drift away, to be thrown into the ocean and forgotten. You were born to live.

-Kala Jordan-Lindsey

You're blessed, so fly like a butterfly, and never give up.

-Kala Jordan-Lindsey

A peace of mind in Christ is free.

-Kala Jordan-Lindsey

Choose yellow. It'll brighten your day.

-Kala Jordan-Lindsey

Writing a book has the power to heal your wounds.

-Kala Jordan-Lindsey

A colorful room comforts your mind.

-Kala Jordan-Lindsey

Waiting is necessary. Be patient.

-Kala Jordan-Lindsey

Sometimes, God will allow you to lose your mind so He can renew your mind.

-Kala Jordan-Lindsey

Hope for better days, and God will let you experience them.

-Kala Jordan-Lindsey

Life without God is more dangerous than crossing a busy street.

-Kala Jordan-Lindsey

The pain you're experiencing now is encouraging to others.

-Kala Jordan-Lindsey

Take care of your heart like Jesus takes care of you.

-Kala Jordan-Lindsey

Living in darkness is a struggle. Choose to live in the Light.

-Kala Jordan-Lindsey

Drinking liquor is powerless and leads to death, so take better care of your health.

-Kala Jordan-Lindsey

An empty bottle is useless if it's not filled with anything, just as a person who's not filled with the Holy Spirit.

-Kala Jordan-Lindsey

It's easy to pray but sometimes more complicated to exercise patience.

-Kala Jordan-Lindsey

Unleash your passion, and you'll be satisfied.

-Kala Jordan-Lindsey

Live, laugh, and love through every test of life.

-Kala Jordan-Lindsey

Sometimes, life will squeeze the hell out of you so you can be filled with the God in you.

-Kala Jordan-Lindsey

Don't argue. Make love.

-Kala Jordan-Lindsey

Your vision board stands out because God is in your plans.

-Kala Jordan-Lindsey

A band-aid treats your wounds, but God has the power to turn your scars into a testimony.

-Kala Jordan-Lindsey

Money talks, but God's love is more powerful.

-Kala Jordan-Lindsey

Hook up with Jesus, and He'll never break up with you.

-Kala Jordan-Lindsey

Get out your head and live, or you'll be miserable.

-Kala Jordan-Lindsey

Get rid of your negative thoughts, and your life will improve.

-Kala Jordan-Lindsey

Stay away from worldly distractions, or you'll get yourself in trouble.

-Kala Jordan-Lindsey

Give with a heart like Jesus.

-Kala Jordan-Lindsey

I'm free, baby.

-Kala Jordan-Lindsey

Life can be challenging but squeeze out a laugh or two in every problematic situation.

-Kala Jordan-Lindsey

The Most Powerful Quotes to Enhance Your Life

Create an environment that's welcoming and brings peace to your heart, like home.

-Kala Jordan-Lindsey

Reading a good book is healthy for your mind. It strengthens a weak or noisy heart.

-Kala Jordan-Lindsey

Be quiet and pray.

-Kala Jordan-Lindsey

The Most Powerful Quotes to Enhance Your Life

Take a selfie with confidence.

-Kala Jordan-Lindsey

Conquer fear with faith and never look back.

-Kala Jordan-Lindsey

Smile with or without money. Life is more than trees.

-Kala Jordan-Lindsey

Lead with faith, not doubt.

-Kala Jordan-Lindsey

Your life is valuable, so make every experience special.

—Kala Jordan-Lindsey

I'm married to the most handsome man on the planet, and I know it.

—Kala Jordan-Lindsey

Every day, you have a choice. Be wise.

—Kala Jordan-Lindsey

The Most Powerful Quotes to Enhance Your Life

*Be inspired to express yourself.
It's fulfilling.*

-Kala Jordan-Lindsey

*Celebrate your life and be
thankful before it vanishes.*

-Kala Jordan-Lindsey

*There's no limit to success. Strive
to accomplish your goals.*

-Kala Jordan-Lindsey

The Most Powerful Quotes to Enhance Your Life

Today is more valuable than your future. Make the most of it.

-Kala Jordan-Lindsey

That storm wasn't so bad after all. God delivered you.

-Kala Jordan-Lindsey

I love my song. I'm free.

-Kala Jordan-Lindsey

Just because it's always been a certain way doesn't mean it will stay that way. Think bigger and have faith.

-Kala Jordan-Lindsey

You lost your job because God wanted you to seek Him and appreciate His grace.

-Kala Jordan-Lindsey

An overflow of joy will constantly flow through your heart when you operate in your calling.

-Kala Jordan-Lindsey

Your dimples are attractive, like my heart.

-Kala Jordan-Lindsey

We live in a dark world, so embrace the mighty Son and the beautiful sun.

-Kala Jordan-Lindsey

Start your own business so that you can mind your own business.

-Kala Jordan-Lindsey

Life is unpredictable, so don't stress over things out of your control. Instead, let God handle your problems.

-Kala Jordan-Lindsey

If God didn't work it out, you wouldn't be here.

-Kala Jordan-Lindsey

You're beautiful in so many ways that you compare to no other person.

-Kala Jordan-Lindsey

There's power in your voice, so embrace it because many have muted theirs.

-Kala Jordan-Lindsey

Discipline your mind to commit to a healthier lifestyle, and you'll start to experience life-changing results.

-Kala Jordan-Lindsey

Treat yourself to a lovely getaway and have the time of your life.

-Kala Jordan-Lindsey

For every loss, expect a gain.

-Kala Jordan-Lindsey

The Most Powerful Quotes to Enhance Your Life

Acknowledgements

First, I would like to thank my Heavenly Father for completing this book. Without His grace, mercy, and mighty strength, it would not have been possible.

To my phenomenal editor, Sana Abuleil, thank you once again for assisting me on the pages of my life and for your incredible gift and support. You rock!

Also, my completion of this book could not have been possible without the love, support, and prayers from my best friend, Belinda A. Dalton. You encouraged me every time with a call, text, or heartfelt card and made me laugh when I needed it the most. Your kind heart is forever appreciated. Love you, Sis! And to my biggest fans and beautiful parents, Jefferson and Evetta, thank you to the moon and back. The countless times you supported me unconditionally will never be forgotten. I love you more than banana pudding!

Finally, to my loving and supportive husband, Anthony, and our precious girls, Kamaria and Tamia: You encouraged me from day one and motivated me with every reason to make it to the finish line. I love you with all my heart. Thank you to my family, friends, and readers. Muah!

The Most Powerful Quotes to Enhance Your Life

Other Books by Kala Jordan-Lindsey

when you rise: Book 2

when you rise: Book 1, Second Edition

when you rise: Book 1

words from the heart- First Edition

Run Your Business in Ten Essentials for 365 Days and Beyond

Please be so kind as to leave a review.

Thank You. God bless.

www.ingramcontent.com/pod-product-compliance
Lightning Source LLC
LaVergne TN
LVHW081347060526
838201LV00050B/1733